A DOGS LIFE

CREATIVE EDUCATION 🐾 CREATIVE PAPERBACKS

Published by Creative Education and Creative Paperbacks
P.O. Box 227, Mankato, Minnesota 56002
Creative Education and Creative Paperbacks
are imprints of The Creative Company
www.thecreativecompany.us

Design and production by Chelsey Luther
Art direction by Rita Marshall
Printed in the United States of America

Photographs by Alamy (fotodezign 8), Getty Images (Pat Gaines/Moment Open, Hillary Kladke/Moment, @Hans Surfer/Moment), iStockphoto (adogslifephoto, fotoedu, FtLaudGirl, IvonneW, jclegg, Kerkez, Liliboas, pearleye, richardwatson, Tinieder), Chelsey Luther, Shutterstock (AmySachar, Aurora72, CNuisin, Fabian Faber, BW Folsom, Ian 2010, V J Matthew, Mega Pixel, MicrostockStudio, Pakhnyushchy, Richard Peterson, Picsfive, George Rudy, SikorskiFotografie, Spasta, Mary Swift, Orapin Thepsuttinun)

Library of Congress Cataloging-in-Publication Data
Names: Rosen, Michael J., author.
Title: Treating your dog / Michael J. Rosen.
Series: A dog's life.
Summary: An instructional guide to training dogs, this title touches on the importance of playing with and rewarding a dog and informs young dog owners what to expect from the loyal, loving animals.
Identifiers: ISBN 978-1-64026-058-0 (hardcover) / ISBN 978-1-62832-646-8 (pbk) / ISBN 978-1-64000-174-9 (eBook)
This title has been submitted for CIP processing under LCCN 2018938984.

CCSS: RI.1.1, 2, 4, 5, 6, 7; RI.2.1, 2, 5, 6, 7; RI.3.1, 5, 7; RF.1.1, 3, 4; RF.2.3, 4

First Edition HC 9 8 7 6 5 4 3 2 1
First Edition PBK 9 8 7 6 5 4 3 2 1

TREATING
Your Dog

CONTENTS

07

If Your Dog Could Read ...

11

The Need for Play

14

When to Treat

18

A Dog's Toy Chest

20

Let's Fetch!

22

Try This: Braided Chew Toy

24

Glossary, Websites, Index

If Your Dog Could Read ...

You will have to read these six books for your dog as well as yourself. You will be both student and teacher. A dog is a fine student—*if* you are a fine teacher!

Your dog will supply his talent to learn. He will work for praise, play, and treats because they create safety, happiness, and comfort.

In this book, you will see how important play is to a dog's life. Toys, games, and treats that follow successful training help keep a dog's mind and body healthy. And they are part of a daily routine that creates a rich companionship.

The Need for Play

Play is key to your dog's well-being. As a pack animal, he has an inborn need to play from the time he is a puppy. Play is a safe way to practice survival skills in the wild—or the neighborhood.

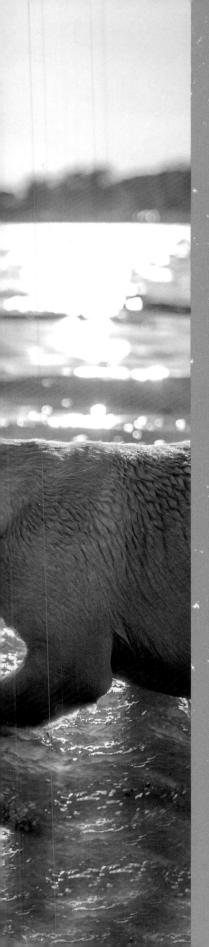

Play keeps a dog's body fit and healthy. It keeps his mind active, too. And play is a great reward during or after training. All your dog truly needs for most of his playtime hours is you! Figure out what skills, games, and habits you can enjoy together.

When to Treat

Use treats *occasionally*. Treats can be useful as part of training, when learning to meet strangers, or when you need to focus the dog's attention. A dog wants to learn for many reasons: it pleases you; it challenges him; his life gets fuller!

To safely give a treat, hold it in your fist. Stand beside, not in front of, your dog. Lower your fist, fingers facing upward, and let the dog sniff. Now quickly open your fist. Keep your fingers and thumb together to form a little plate. This makes it easy for your dog to take the treat.

You can also give the treat from a squatting position. Place the back of your fist on the ground. Have your dog sniff your hand. Open it up, flattening your fingers against the ground.

A Dog's Toy Chest

Every dog needs toys to call his own. Puppies, in particular, need acceptable things to chew. Otherwise, they will teethe on other objects. Avoid toys that are:

- colored with paint that can flake off;
- made of anything that can be chewed into large pieces and swallowed;
- small enough to fit entirely inside the mouth (such as a golf ball).

Tennis balls and Frisbees are perfect for catching and fetching. Rugged squeaking toys and rubber toys that are hard to break are good for chewing.

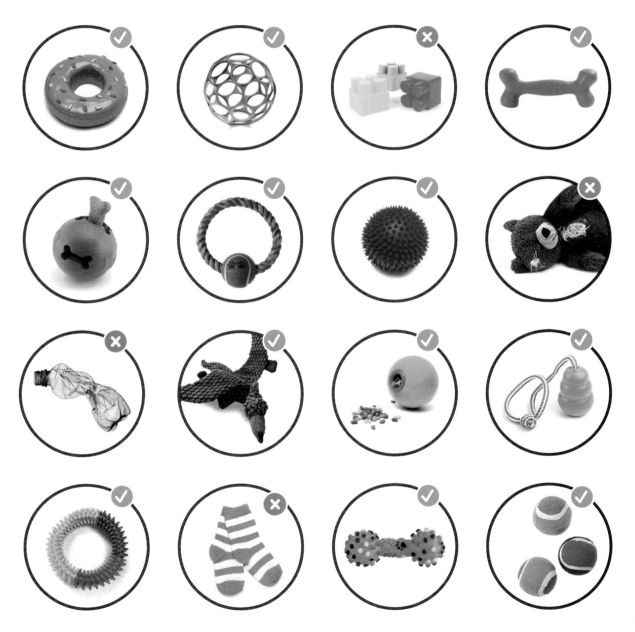

Let's Fetch!

A fetching game can be played by chasing a dog after he has caught the ball. Other times, the dog seems to say, "I got it, brought it back, and dropped it at your feet. Now throw it again!"

Try a simple game of catch: toss a ball across the yard or into the air. Or roll or bounce the ball across the ground. Play keep-away with one friend or a circle of friends.

Frequently give the dog a chance with the ball.

Braided Chew Toy

Give your dog some tug-o'-war fun with this homemade toy. You need three equal-length pieces of thick fabric, such as corduroy, denim, or terrycloth. Shape the toy to fit your dog's size: shorter/thinner for smaller dogs or longer/thicker for larger dogs.

1 Knot the strips together at one end.

2 Braid the strips together tightly:

    A First, place the right piece over the middle one.

    B Then place the left piece over the middle one.

    C Repeat this pattern along the length of the fabric.

3 Leave enough unbraided to create a second knot.

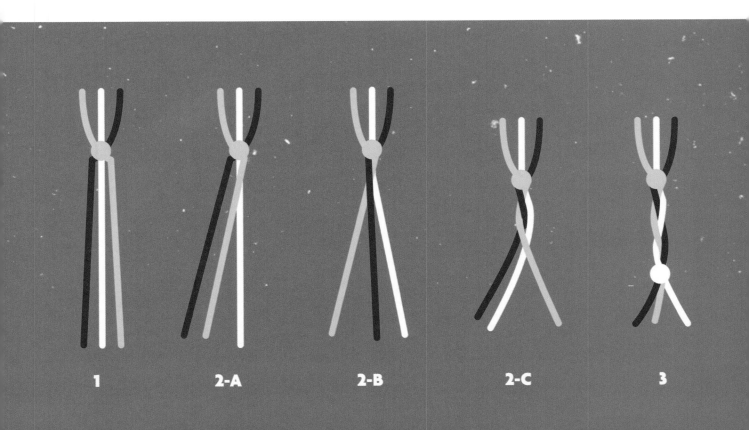

1   2-A   2-B   2-C   3

Glossary

inborn: a natural feeling or ability that exists from birth

routine: a fixed set of actions that is repeated regularly

rugged: tough, strong, or durable

teethe: to grow teeth; teething puppies often chew on hard objects

Websites

American Kennel Club: Dog Training Basics
http://www.akc.org/content/dog-training/basics/
Pick up tips for training your dog.

PBS Kids: Dog Games
http://pbskids.org/games/dog/
Play dog games with PBS show characters to learn more about the animals.

Index

games 8, 13, 20
learning 7, 14
playing 7, 8, 11, 13
puppies 11, 18
rewards 7, 13
teaching 7
teething 18
toys 8, 18–19, 20, 22
training 8, 13, 14
treats 7, 8, 14, 16–17